WHERE

I'M COMING FROM

The Year In Review: 2010

WHERE
I'M COMING FROM
The Year In Review

⌘

IMAM ZAID SHAKIR

Zaid Shakir

N D™
publishers

Where I'm Coming From: 2010
Zaid Shakir

NID Publishers
PO Box 2895
Antioch, CA 94531
(510) 387-2604

Library of Congress Control Number: 2011285300
ISBN-13: 978-0-9792281-8-6

Manufactured in the United States of America

Cover design by Susanah I. Pittam

CONTENTS

INTRODUCTION

The past year has been a trying one for Muslims in the United States. The steady drone of anti-Islamic sentiment, growing since the tragic events of September 11, 2001, was catalyzed by a series of unfortunate incidents. We could mention among them the Fort Hood shootings, the failed attempt to detonate a bomb aboard an American-bound aircraft over Detroit, Michigan, the failed bomb attempt at Times Square in New York, the manufactured controversy surrounding the "Ground Zero Mosque" and the "Qur'an burning" event organized by a nondescript Florida pastor. Collectively, these and other events helped to amplify the voices of anti-Islamic bigots to a sometimes frightening pitch.

The challenges facing Muslims have not been confined to the words of bigots, racists, pundits, polemicists and "shock jocks." The physical violence visited on Muslims by the United States war machine in places like Afghanistan, Pakistan and Yemen has intensified. The number of civilian casualties, in what has been dubbed the war on terror, continue to mount. This latter development has deep strategic implications for relations between America and the Muslim world.

In addition to the damage meted out by Hellfire rockets, five-hundred pound bombs and Bradley fighting vehicles, Muslims have increasingly been the victims of the reckless and ill-conceived actions of their coreligionists. Bombings in mosques and marketplaces have become a sad fact of everyday life in some Muslim cities. Here in the United States, there seems to be an overabundance of misguided Muslims whose ignorance, stupidity or maliciousness leads them to be willing participants in increasingly elaborate entrapment schemes, which only serve to deepen the growing animosity many feel towards Islam and Muslims. That animosity only makes it easier for anti-Muslim demagogues to arouse nativistic passions that lend support to policies that are potentially catastrophic, both to this country and the Muslim world.

During the past year, I have written essays in response to many of the issues referred to above. Some have been posted on my website, www.newislamicdirections.com, while others were written for *Emel Magazine*, a groundbreaking British monthly. They were also featured on that magazine's website. As I reflected on many of those essays, it occurred to me that they might be worth gathering into a single printed volume. That volume might prove beneficial to readers who are looking for insight into the ideas and personalities shaping the news, especially those readers who are not exposed to an Islamic perspective on the events of the day.

The decision to move forward with the humble project of gathering some of those writings into a printed volume is the origin of this book, *Where I'm Coming From: 2010*. It is my hope that I will be able to issue a similar collection on an annual basis as part of an ongoing series. For now, let us look back on the past year through these reflections. Hopefully, doing so will prove an enriching experience.

Imam Zaid Shakir

11/16/10

1.

REMEMBERING
IMAM LUQMAN ABDULLAH

On Wednesday, October 28, 2009, Imam Luqman Abdullah, a humble servant of America's underclass, was killed by a fusillade of bullets fired by government agents, some of whom had played an integral role in helping to stage the crimes he was accused of committing. His story, like that of all humans, is a complicated one. Unfortunately, most people in this country will never learn of the real Imam Luqman Abdullah. The complexity of his life will be drowned out by the simplistic images of the homegrown Muslim extremist –a caricature.

The nuances of his story, his dedication to family, friends, and community; and his struggle to live a dignified life despite the crushing weight of poverty, will all be lost. With their loss, America loses yet another opportunity to attain a small part of the understanding so vital to move this country towards the sort of policies it needs to pursue, both domestically and internationally, if it is to avoid the consuming trap of imperial hubris and the inevitable ravages of her twin, who is never too far behind -Nemesis.

Imam Luqman was not a fan of the American government. It is difficult to find many people living and working in one of the most impoverished neighborhoods in Detroit, one of the poorest cities in this country, who are fans of the government –regardless of their religious beliefs. Too much of the country's sordid underbelly is exposed in such communities to engender much affection for its government. Too many souls are lost to the liquor that flows too freely. Too many lives are fractured by crack and other debilitating drugs. Too many dreams are deferred by the crushing combination of impoverished schools, dysfunctional families, and insufficient opportunities and services –in housing, employment, and healthcare. And far, far too many people are gunned down by the bullets flying too freely from guns that are too easily available. In most instances the trigger is pulled by the brown or black hand of a lost soul hailing from the same neighborhood as the victim, but in far too many instances it is pulled by an agent of the state.

Imam Luqman knew that violence well, on both ends. He was shot and nearly killed by a robber who assailed his vehicle during a time when he was a struggling cab driver. His life finally came to a grisly end at the hands of government agents who had lured him to the warehouse where he was gunned down after allegedly shooting a dog that had been unleashed against him.

However, despite the poverty, the pressure, and the pain existing in communities such as these, there are heartwarming stories of human dignity and decency. Imam Luqman Abdullah was the author of many of these stories. He wrote them with his service to the community, the people he assisted, day in and day out, such as providing transport to people lacking vehicles, arranging for a heater to be repaired before the onslaught of a brutal Detroit winter, and in countless other ways. He also wrote them in his commitment to his family. The Imam has thirteen children. Not all of them are his biological children, but all of them affectionately call him Abu, or Papa, because of the sincere advice and guidance he had provided them over the years. He loved his community and his family, and he also loved his religion.

Imam Luqman loved Islam. One who has not experienced the intensity of conversion may not appreciate the depth of that love. Many will point to that intensity as one of the factors feeding what is viewed as a brooding radicalism among African American Muslims. However, for every African American Muslim who has, in an unprovoked manner, done something to harm the interests of this state, hundreds of thousands struggle to improve their own lives and those of their communities. These lives have been removed from the ranks of the living dead and ushered into the ranks of the morally and spiritually quickened, and these revived lives have contributed immensely to the betterment of this country.

For the likes of Imam Luqman, Islam provides a vision for a new and better life. It showed him, and legions of others, how to live. For many African Americans, this is something that the country herself still cannot do. Despite the tremendous progress made in some facets of race relations in this country, it is regrettable that the deep musings of Richard Wright, found at the end of his powerful classic, *Black Boy*, are as relevant today, for many, as they were when penned several decades ago:

> Well, what had I got out of living in the city? What had I got out of living in the South? What had I got out of living in America? I paced the floor, knowing that all I possessed were words and dim knowledge that my country had shown me no examples of how to live a human life. All my life I had been full of a hunger for a new way to live...

Through Islam, Luqman Abdullah and countless others have found a new way to live. It is unfortunate that many seem to prefer the aimless degeneracy that afflicts so many in this country over a life of devotion and service motivated by Islam.

The fiery political rhetoric sometimes employed by the Imam has led his detractors to argue that he was responsible for his own death. After all, they falsely argue, he was an advocate for a violent Islamic revolution in this country. However, those close to the Imam present another picture. They say that his vision of Islam was far removed from any grandiose delusions of overthrowing the American government. His was a vision of creating a space where children could play and flourish free from the influence of drugs, consumerism and the ever-present threat of violence, where young men could grow up without being stalked by the pernicious spectre of gangs and gang warfare, and where families could establish networks of mutual support and assistance. If his neighborhood in Detroit could have been cleaned up to the degree that such conditions prevailed, then that neighborhood would have become Islamic in his view.

One could debate the Imam's political ideology, just as one could debate if the Imam would have ever been moved to a point where he would have become involved, unprovoked, in an act of violence against the state. However, if agents of the state had not infiltrated his mosque and set in motion the series of regrettable events that culminated in his death he would still be alive today. That is a fact beyond dispute.

It would have been inspiring if the agents who had entered his community also brought access to the resources needed to make the healthy community he envisioned a reality. They would have found the strongest ally in Imam Luqman. Instead, they brought intrigue, violence and yet more social devastation. Unfortunately, this is something they had to do, as they were fighting a war on terror. Although Imam Luqman had not been implicated in any terrorist related charges or conspiracies, he would become an unsuspecting victim of that war. In that sense, he is not alone.

In a final, but telling twist to his story, his life came to an end because he allegedly fired the shots that would kill Freddy, the government dog that had been unleashed against him. As his own bullet-riddled body lay handcuffed in a pool of blood on that cold, hard Detroit-area warehouse floor, Freddy was evacuated by helicopter to a hospital for potentially life-saving treatment. People familiar with communities like those Imam Luqman lived and worked in are not surprised by the prioritization of beast over human. As the popular singing group, The Temptations, worded it, "...*it's an everyday thing, in the ghetto.*"

2.

RESPONDING TO THE FORT HOOD TRAGEDY

❦

This is my response to the Fort Hood tragedy and events both associated with it and ensuing from it. I begin by expressing my deepest condolences to the families of all of the dead and wounded. There is no legitimate reason for their deaths, just as I firmly believe there is no legitimate reason for the deaths of the hundreds of thousands of Iraqi and Afghani civilians who have perished as a result of those two conflicts. Even though I disagree with the continued prosecution of those wars, and even though I believe that the US war machine is the single greatest threat to world peace, I must commend the top military brass at Fort Hood, and President Obama for encouraging restraint and for refusing to attribute the crime allegedly perpetrated by Major Nidal Malik Hasan to Islam. We pray that God blesses us to see peace and sanity prevail during these tense times.

Introduction

One of the greatest foundations of Islam is truth. One of the ninety-nine names of God is *al-Haqq* (the Truth). It is impermissible to distort the truth, to present falsehood as fact, or to present half-truths as definitive declarations. Truth, along with Goodness and Beauty are the three great transcendental realities that Islam and all other religions exhort us to both realize and actualize in our lives. In the Arabic/Islamic lexicon these are known as *al-Haqq* (the Truth), *al-Ihsan* (Goodness), and *al-Jamaal* (Beauty).

Concerning the truth, our Prophet, peace and blessings upon him, taught us to pray, *Allahumma Arinal Haqqa Haqqan wa Zurqnat Tiba'ahu,* "O God! Show us the truth as truth and bless us to follow it." The Qur'an presents the truth as a powerful, self-evident reality that is distinguishable from falsehood without any need for extraneous clarification (2:256). The mere presence of the truth is enough to dispel the clouds of darkness and falsehood (17:81). Therefore, a great objective of our religion is discovering and then following, the truth.

One of the unfortunate consequences of tragic and highly emotive events like the shootings that occurred at Fort Hood, Texas, is that such events are used to advance agendas that by their very nature make a mockery of the truth. This event is no exception. There are those who seek to use this event to portray the Muslim community in this country as an inherent menace whose very existence has to be challenged. Traveling the length and breadth of this country in the service of that community, I know that this is not the truth. The Muslim community in this country is a peace-loving, law-abiding community that has in ways great and small advanced the general welfare of this nation and its citizenry. To present it otherwise is a blatant lie.

Like any other community that has a fairly large percentage of immigrants amongst its members, the Muslim community does have those elements, especially older members or those newly arrived from the Muslim world, whose strongest sentiments, emotional and cultural attachments may be inclined towards the lands they have come from, rather than to the nation they find themselves in. This is true for many members of most immigrant populations. However, generally speaking, such attachments are not found among Muslims born and raised here; nor do they translate into animosity towards or a desire to do harm to this country.

Saying that is not to deny the existence of Muslims who may be agitated by the injustices and inequities they find in American foreign policy, or the increasingly prejudicial or even racist attitudes being advanced by some parties towards America's Muslims. Among them is a small minority whose anger and frustration may render them vulnerable to the appeal of demagogues who would attempt to exploit their emotions to advance a nefarious agenda. In some incidences, a number of psychological factors may converge in their lives pushing them towards acts of violence against their fellow citizens. This might prove to be the case for Major Nidal Malik Hasan, who has been identified as the shooter at Fort Hood, and for a few other random individuals. However, it is not and never will be anything that can even begin to approach the norm in the Muslim community.

There are those who will argue that the problem is those random "few" Muslims who may snap at any time. That is certainly a problem. However, if the recent history of this country is any indication, those few have been less in number and responsible for far less carnage than the "few" from the non-Muslim population. These include postal workers, high school and university students and other random individuals who have snapped and gone on to wreak havoc in our society. One of the great tragedies in this situation is to view the crime Major Hasan is being accused of, as a specifically Muslim problem. It is a human problem and if it is approached as such, perhaps we can learn something from it that will help us to get to the roots of the violent outbursts that are becoming increasingly widespread in our society.

What is unequivocally true is that such violent outbursts that involve attacks against the lives or property of American citizens in this country have nothing to do with Islam. There are no teachings from the normative corpus of Muslim political writings that allow a Muslim to violate the security of the public square, to endanger the lives of the general public, to attack non-combatant civilians, even in a battlefield situation, or to aggress against soldiers who are not in a battlefield. This is especially true where Muslims have entered into an explicit or implicit covenant of protection from non-Muslim political authorities and constitute a distinct minority in a particular land.

Much of the balance of this article will be dedicated to presenting Islamic teachings that substantiate what I have mentioned above concerning the duties of Muslims to protect the public square in any non-Muslim land they may live in or visit, and those teachings that warn against foolhardy, ill-conceived attacks that only bring harm and hardship to innocent, unsuspecting people, Muslims among them.

My argument is a direct refutation of Muslim demagogues who seek to distort Islamic teachings to motivate ignorant Muslims to undertake ill-advised and unsanctioned actions against the citizenry of this country. It is also a refutation of demagogues from other faiths who would maliciously use events such as that occurring at Fort Hood to instigate hatred against innocent Muslims who have nothing to do with what transpired at Fort Hood or similar isolated events. What is mentioned below is nothing new. It is simply a restatement of what I have previously taught.[1]

No Room for Vigilante Treachery in the Divine Law

In his expansive work, *al-Jihad wa'l Qital fi al-Siyasa al-Shar'iyya* (Sanctioned Warfare and Fighting in the Divine Law) Muhammad Khayr Haykal mentions, concerning the implications accruing from an oath of protection:[2]

> The cessation of hostilities that is mentioned here might be a consequence of an oath of protection given by non-Muslims to Muslims, or a consequence of an oath of protection given by Muslims to non-Muslims. In both cases, it obligates a cessation of hostilities against the members of the opposing community who might technically be at war with the

Muslims. [This is so] whether the Muslims have granted the oath of protection or it has been granted to them.[3]

He adds:

It is not permissible for Muslims who have been granted an oath of protection from members of other communities to launch into fighting them, because this is treachery.[4]

Two concepts are critical in what Haykal mentions here, one is the idea of treachery, and the other is the idea of reciprocity. Islam is predicated on honorable behavior. It is the height of dishonor to violate the trust that is extended to a person given the right to move about freely in a particular land based on the assumption that that person has accepted the responsibility to protect and preserve public order in that land and the lives and property of its people.

In his commentary on *al-Mughni*, one of the definitive compendiums of Islamic law according to the Hanbali rite, Imam al-Maqdisi mentions in this regard, "If an oath of protection is given to an enemy population, it is forbidden to fight them, usurp their wealth, or to expose them to any harm."[5] Imam al-Shafi'i clarifies that this includes Muslims who have entered into a non-Muslim land. He states, "If a group of Muslims enter the land of non-Muslims with an oath of protection, the others are safe from them [...] they have no right to oppress or betray them."[6]

Hence, it should be clear that a Muslim is not allowed to aggress against non-Muslims as long as he or she resides in their lands under their protection. Any aggression from their quarter is unsanctioned treachery. If they feel they can no longer accept the perceived or real abuses or injustices of the host people then they are obliged to leave that land if remaining there would push them into acts of violence or aggression against the host community.

The idea of reciprocity is critical in this particular area of inquiry. All of our major legal texts discuss this idea. It is the idea that the responsibilities expected of non-Muslims minorities in Muslim lands are incumbent on Muslims in non-Muslim lands. Hence, just as it would be unacceptable for a non-Muslim residing in a Muslim land to attack the people of that land, civilian or military, it is unacceptable for a Muslim residing in a non-Muslim land to engage in similar acts. This is an undeniable principle in our law. Hence, respecting it is not a stratagem or a convenient contingency; it is upholding an inviolable principle.

It is also well-known amongst Muslim scholars that it is prohibited to undertake any acts that will result in widespread harm returning to Muslims. This is based on the prophetic hadith, "There is no initiating or reciprocating harm."[7] This hadith has given rise to the legal maxim, "Harm is to be removed." Hence, any action that is likely to result in widespread harm to Muslims is unsanctioned.

In the current political climate in America where the demonizing of Muslims has evolved into an industry, and where rules of civility and the rejection of any meaningful anti-defamation statutes allow for indiscriminate calls to murder Muslims on public airwaves, it is clear that individuals that violate these codes of conduct are grievously harming both Muslims and non-Muslims alike. In this era, in which Mosques and other Muslim organizations are infiltrated by agent provocateurs who encourage some susceptible Muslim individuals to engage in acts that could potentially unleash waves of anti-Muslim venom, it is clear to anyone with a modicum of intellect that attacks such as the one that occurred at Fort Hood have no Islamic sanction, neither in principle nor from a tactical point of view.

Such attacks only give credence to those foul elements who desire to justify ongoing wars against Muslim populations. There are self-proclaimed muftis and so-called scholars in the Muslim world who think that by calling for such attacks they can draw America into deeper involvements in places such as Iraq or Afghanistan which will become America's "next Vietnam." Little do they realize that they are encouraging elements that would bomb Afghan towns and villages with the same insane impunity that was visited upon places such as Tokyo, Dresden, Hamburg and Berlin during World War II. These so-called scholars apparently fail to realize that here in the West a growing number of people are arguing that Islam poses an existential threat to America and western civilization. One of the few things giving any credence to these perverse arguments are belligerent actions, which can be attributed to Muslims.

Ibn Juzayy mentions in al-Qawa'id al-Fiqhiyya:

> If the Muslims know that they will be slaughtered in whole-sale fashion it is fitting that they abandon fighting. If they know that they will be slaughtered and that their losses will do little to alter the strategic balance vis-à-vis the enemy forces, it is absolutely obligatory that they abandon any encounter.[8]

Any Muslim who thinks that an unsanctioned act of violence he may undertake in this country is going to alter the strategic balance is grandly deluded or inexcusably ignorant. His undertaking any violent act in this country is additionally forbidden because he is likely going to be killed, gravely injured, or captured in the encounter. Imam al-Shawkani mentions in al-*Sayl al-Jarrar*, "It is well-known legal reasoning that one who strikes out [against an enemy] knowing beforehand that he will be killed, captured or vanquished, has hurled himself to destruction."[9] Imam al-Shawkani explains that such an act is forbidden based on the Qur'anic verse, *Do not hurl yourself to destruction with your own hand.* (2:195)[10] This argument, which discourages foolhardy acts of desperation based on this verse, is also made by Ibn 'Abideen in his commentary on *al-Durr al-Mukhtar*.[11]

There is another salient point that we must mention in this context. No one, even in a Muslim land, has the right to undertake violent acts, even against a recognized enemy when the political authorities of that land determine that those acts will incur harm to Muslims [or other innocent people]. Dr. Haykal elaborates on this point at length:

> The lawful authorities in a land possess the right, and this right is similarly conferred by valid legislative principles, to absolutely prevent any method, or any organization whose very nature would result in consequences that would expose

the Muslims to grave danger and harm. Therefore, when the legislative authorities perceive that something that may originally be permissible has consequences that involve any degree of harm, it is their responsibility to prevent that harm. Rather, it is incumbent on them to prevent it. This is accomplished by preventing individuals from arming themselves and preventing them from forming armed militias that are independent of the standing army. Indeed, the divine law has given the authorities a number of legislative principles to use in order to cut off any path where the winds of harm may blow from.[12]

If this is the case for a Muslim country, how can it be permissible to engage in vigilante acts and underground militias in a non-Muslim land where Muslims are forbidden to threaten public order or to independently implement any Islamic teachings related to strategic affairs?

Finally, as implied above, Muslim leaders have the responsibility to protect the faithful from foolhardy acts that will lead to unnecessary loss of life, and to warn them again individuals who would lead them towards such acts. For this reason, 'Umar bin al-Khattab, warned against reckless commanders who would expose the faithful to unnecessary hardship. This led to him advising his governors, "Do not appoint al-Bara' ibn Malik over any Muslim army."[13]

This warning was issued owing to al-Bara's known recklessness and his lack of consideration of the consequences of his actions for his troops. It is a shame that we find those who pass themselves off as Muslim scholars riding roughshod over the Shari'ah in ways that recklessly and insensitively endanger innocent Muslims and non-Muslims alike. It is incumbent that such individuals are shunned by the Muslims of this country, and their ignorance of the divine law exposed. This is especially true if they are not on the ground in this country and are therefore not attuned to the nature of the struggles and vulnerabilities of our community.

Conclusion

So what are the Muslims of this country to do in the aftermath of the tragedy at Fort Hood? We have to carry on doing the good things we were doing before it occurred. Indeed, we need to increase that good. Our civil rights can be assailed, we can be denied equal protection under the law, our lawful and law-abiding organizations can be closed down, but no one can take our dignity from us, no one can prevent us from being decent neighbors, honest workers, dedicated students, faithful citizens, and pious believers. Furthermore, no one can prevent us from using the constitutional and legal means available to us to seek the redress of our grievances.

Certainly, the heightened levels of hate speech, the whispers of a coming backlash, and elected officials who have gone on record promising to do nothing to mitigate such a backlash are all unsettling. However, if we preserve and remain ever mindful of the wise commandments that are available to guide our steps, we should rest assured that God will not abandon us. He states in the Qur'an, "You will surely be tested in your property and your persons. And you will hear from [some of] those given the Scripture before you, and from the idolaters much abuse. If you patiently persevere, and remain mindful of God, surely this is a manifestation of prophetic resolution." (3:186)

At this time when very powerful and well-financed interests are rallying against us; at this time when we can entertain no real hope of meaningful support from any Muslim country, we have to redouble our dependence on God; we have to live for Him and seek our strength through Him. "Whoever remains mindful of God, He makes for him a way out, He bestows His sustenance upon him from directions he could never imagine, and one who places his trust in God finds that He suffices him…" (65:2-3) This is the way of the Prophets, peace be upon them. Let it be our way.

3.

GRAVEYARD DETROIT

Detroit, Michigan is an historic American city. From its humble roots as a French trading post in the early 18th century, it grew to become one of the largest cities in the United States. It was nearly burned to the ground in 1805, and was scorched by the flames of race riots in 1863, 1943 and 1967. During the 20th century, its fate has waxed and waned with the rise and fall of the American auto industry. However, despite its travails, the city has displayed resiliency and has witnessed a comeback of sorts in recent years with the renewal of its downtown and riverfront areas, at least before the great financial melt-down of 2008.

A graveyard is a place where physically dead bodies are interred. This is its literal meaning. However, the word graveyard also has a figurative meaning. It means a place where worn-out or obsolete equipment or objects are kept. This meaning can be stretched to include a depository of worn-out ideas. In this latter sense, recent events have conspired to render Detroit a graveyard, representing the end of worn out, expired and discredited ideas.

Among them we may include the idea that for African Americans, the North represented an improvement over the conditions that prevailed in the South; the idea that major American corporations, despite their firm commitment to the bottom line, are the engines of economic growth and prosperity for the masses of working people; the idea that there is an inherent "Islamic" threat that challenges the hegemony of a militarized American state; and the idea that extremist "Islamist" violence can possibly secure any good whatsoever for Muslim people and their causes.

The Myth of the "Promised Land"

Many African Americans viewed the North as a mythical "promised land." The racist terrorism of the Ku Klux Klan, the Red Shirts, the White League and similar groups, which was almost omnipresent in the South, was absent from the large cities of the North. Furthermore, factory work promised relatively high paying jobs, free from the vagaries of the oppressive farms of the South where work, in many instances, amounted to legalized slavery. For many black folks, Detroit epitomized the promise of the North. They found plentiful work in the burgeoning factories springing up around the city's auto industry. As a result, through the middle decades of the 20th century, an expanding black middle class would gradually leave a widening imprint on the social, cultural and political life of the city.

Detroit's black middle class would contribute intellectual giants such as Reverend C.L. Franklin to America's civil rights struggle. Individuals such as the boxer Joe Louis, Franklin's daughter, Aretha, and the many recording artists of Barry Gordy's Motown Records became American cultural icons. The prosperity of Detroit's black middle class in the 1940s and 1950s, was symbolized by "Paradise Valley" and its scores of black-owned establishments such as the elegant Gotham Hotel.

However, the overwhelming majority of black folks migrating to Detroit did not find heaven in the North. They were housed in dirty, dilapidated slums as racially segregated as any southern neighborhood. Fluctuating economic cycles and the gradual exodus of manufacturing jobs led to high unemployment rates that would aggravate tensions between the new arrivals and more established white workers. Tens of thousands would never find meaningful employment or decent housing.

The harsh economic realities of life in the North were worsened by difficult social realities. Crammed into dilapidated ghettos, cut off from the safety net of their extended southern families, denied access to higher education that was available in the historical black colleges and universities that had been established in the South: Howard, Morehouse, Fisk, Tuskegee etc.—many sought refuge in readily available drugs such as heroin, or cocaine and alcohol.

The highways built in the 1950s, the construction of one, Interstate 75, led to the bulldozing of Paradise Valley, facilitated the massive white flight of the 1950s and 1960s from Detroit to now accessible distant suburbs and the flight of the black middle class from the inner-city areas to the abandoned white neighborhoods.

These developments, culminated in the destructive riots of 1967 with over 2,500 structures destroyed and rendering Detroit the symbolic graveyard of the "Promised Land" ideal that had attracted so many black people to the North. Its tombstones are the blocks of burned out and decaying buildings and homes. Many of these areas have been abandoned and ravaged giving parts of inner-city Detroit the look and feel of Berlin or Tokyo after the firebombing of those cities.

The obituary of that buried dream was twice written, both times in Detroit, in July 1984 and a decade later in August 1994. In the former month, Reverend C.L. Franklin, who had fallen into a coma after being shot during a robbery of his home five years earlier, died; on the latter date, Rosa Parks, whose heroic defiance had ignited the heroic African American civil rights struggle, was robbed and beaten in her Detroit home. The dream they represented was no longer deferred; in Detroit, it was dead.

As GM Goes, So Goes the Nation

The Detroit auto industry represented a different type of dream for another set of people: the white middle class. Karl Marx, posited that capitalism, and the bourgeoisie it disproportionately benefitted, would collapse in the face of a massive worker or proletariat revolution brought on by the systematic expansion and impoverishment of the laboring class, and the equally systematic shrinking and enrichment of the owing class.

The emergence of the Detroit auto industry in the early years of the 20th century, catapulted by management and production techniques introduced by Frederick Winslow Taylor and Henry Ford, would lead to levels of proficiency and scales of production that facilitated the popularization of easily affordable automobiles and unimagined profits. During the middle decades of the 20th century, increasingly larger shares of those profits would find their way into the pockets of laborers, owing in large part to the unionizing efforts of the AFL-CIO and its sometimes estranged sister, the UAW (AFL –American Federation of Labor; CIO –Congress of Industrial Organizations; UAW –United Auto Workers).

The unionized auto industry, largely serving a white constituency, would never know the kind of revolutionary upheavals Marx and others had predicted. The white middle class emerging in Detroit not only escaped the collective misery Marx had envisioned for workers, but the automobile and its associated mobility, lifestyle and the restructuring of urban and rural spaces led to the creation of an entirely different and deceptively enticing way of life: suburbia.

It is not coincidental that suburbia, and the deeply fragmented, alienated, compartmentalized and racially segregated lifestyle it encouraged, would be most startlingly illustrated in the vicinity of Detroit, home of the auto industry that drove white flight nationwide.

"Whitopia," a mythical land where home ownership, having become the signal designator for attaining the American dream,is a place where the poverty of "menacing" black folks, and the perceived or real criminality it breeds, seemed a distant reality left for others to deal with. In that land of alienating affluence, consumerist passions, fueled by the salaries gifted to workers by decades of unionizing, could be freely engaged -first in the strip malls that littered the suburban landscape, and later in huge self-enclosed mega-malls.

Unfortunately, labor's victory would prove ephemeral. The auto industry, colluding with big oil, would pay little heed to fuel efficiency. When global economic conditions led to exponential increases in fuel prices, American gas guzzlers could not compete with far more fuel efficient and increasingly better-made foreign cars, especially Japanese vehicles. The rising strength of the Japanese and European auto industries and the ever larger slices of both the American and global markets they were able to win from their American rivals, led to declining profits and accelerating numbers of layoffs and plant closures in the States.

During the 1980s and 1990s unions were forced to give back many of the hard-earned benefits they had garnered for workers. Those workers who still had jobs in the auto industry found themselves struggling to make ends meet. Meanwhile, the Detroit-based automakers were seduced by the influx of bogus wealth into the American financial system during the late 1990s and the first few years of the 21st Century. Encouraged by the liberal policies of Bill Clinton, epitomized by his gutting of the Glass-Steagall Act, the automakers banked on the continued popularity of energy inefficient, but highly profitable sports utility vehicles (SUVs). However, in the wake of steadily rising fuel prices beginning in 2003 and the financial meltdown of 2008, the demand for SUVs collapsed and with it the vestiges of the Detroit-based American auto industry as a dominant international force.

That twin collapse, automotive and financial, was a deathblow to the "Whitopia" surrounding Detroit. Thousands of homes were sold at a loss as their owners packed up and ironically headed south.

Thousands of others fell into foreclosure as their owners walked away; abandoning their properties to the rapacious banks that encouraged their purchase through levels of manipulation and mendacity that have not been witnessed in this country since the era of the 19th Century robber barons.

With the collapse of the Detroit auto industry, and the refusal of a government that had given trillions of dollars to bailout the banking and financial sectors to save it, the idea that big business would be the engine pushing the prosperity of the American, mostly white, middle class has died. Like the African American dream of a promised land, its graveyard is Detroit. Its tombstones are the rusting factories in and around the city, and the acres of abandoned parking lots spotted with weeds cracking through the lonely blacktop deserts they have become; and the vacated, puddle-splattered, unfinished concrete foundations and weed filled lots of distant suburban developments started at the height of the lively housing bubble in 2005-2006, now given up for dead.

The Menace of "Islamic" Terrorism

Detroit is also the graveyard of the fabricated idea of the menacing Islamic enemy. That there is a threat of a minuscule percentage of deranged, alienated, suicidal or sinister Muslims engaging in acts of mindless terror that threaten the lives of an even more miniscule percentage of Americans is undeniable. However, the idea that there is a strategically significant Islamic threat possessing any significant resources that can be translated into the kind of power that can threaten a militarized America or its global financial empire is a baseless fiction.

It is fitting that Detroit should figure heavily in any real or symbolic developments involving Islam in America. It was in Detroit that the Nation of Islam (NOI), the largest and most successful movement associated with Islam in America, was born. Detroit was also the city in which Malcolm X would first rise to prominence as a talented young minister in the NOI. Malcolm would later move to Harlem and achieve international stature as the national spokesman for the leader of the NOI, Elijah Muhammad, and then as an independent voice for both Sunni Muslims and black liberation.

The killing of Imam Luqman Abdullah, a Muslim activist based in one of the poorest neighborhoods in Detroit exposes the existential terrorist fiction. Imam Luqman was allegedly the leader of a group of radical, separatist-minded Muslims whose potential danger warranted the infiltration and surveillance of their mosque, entrapping them in an elaborate scheme involving stolen property and finally the ambush and brutal slaughter of the Imam.

The entire operation exposes the fictitious and empty nature of the Islamic threat. While it is true Imam Luqman was known to engage in fierce anti-American rhetoric, what actual capabilities did he and his followers possess? Their mosque, in one of the poorest sections of Detroit is in serious disrepair and threatened with foreclosure. The state of the mosque alone begs the question, "How could a group so poor that they could barely afford to operate a small mosque in one of the poorest neighborhoods in America overthrow the United States government or establish a separate state anywhere on American soil?" The answer is obvious except to those whose minds are so poisoned by their narrow, self-serving racist agenda that they cannot see reality for what it is.

Hence, when Imam Luqman was gunned down by a fusillade of bullets unleashed by an unknown number of agents, the real nature of the threat he represents was exposed. Even if he did possess a single firearm, as it is alleged, what threat did he represent in the face of the fully automatic high caliber arsenal in the hands of the bulletproof vested, shielded, numerically superior forces arrayed against him? None. Extrapolate from that situation to the global confrontation between America and "radical" Islam and you will understand the true nature of the "Islamic" threat.

Hence, with the brutal murder of Imam Luqman, Detroit is once again a symbolic graveyard. In it is buried the idea of the existential Islamic threat. Its tombstones are the tiny mosque Imam Luqman once headed and the cold warehouse in nearby Dearborn where he was gunned down and left to die like a rabid dog, while Freddy, the dog he allegedly shot, was airlifted from the scene by helicopter.

The Glorious "Jihad"

Finally, Detroit is a graveyard for the idea that "Islamic" terrorism can secure any benefit for the Muslim people. That idea fizzled as surely as the bomb allegedly hidden in Farouk Abdul Mutallab's underwear fizzled –an unexploded, unspectacular, unmitigated disaster. Saying that is not to deny the possibility of a Muslim lunatic engaging in an act of violence against innocent people in this country. However, the idea of a well organized, global network of "jihadists" capable of serving as anything other than a pitiful justification for this country's inability to come to grips with its self-eroding militarism is as pathetic as Farouk's underwear bomb.

In the aftermath of that disaster we are left to ask, "What benefit would have accrued to Muslims had that bomb exploded, murdering three hundred unsuspecting, innocent passengers in American airspace on Christmas Day?" None! Instead, an exponentially larger number of unsuspecting, innocent Muslims than those already experiencing American-style justice would have bombs and rockets raining down on their towns, hamlets and villages. An exponentially larger numbers of innocent Muslims than those already herded into dungeons scattered around the world would be hauled off to be tortured and brutalized into confessing their membership in phantom organizations or their complicity in crimes they have no knowledge of.

Had that bomb exploded, the heroic actions of everyday Muslims resisting the occupation of their lands, the usurpation of their resources, and rankled by the murders and humiliation of their countrymen and women would be callously dismissed as wanton "terrorism." Even American individuals sympathetic to the plight of those under occupation and siege would be rendered insensitive by the coldblooded action of a clearly disturbed stranger with no connection to the Muslims who would have been left to bear the consequences of his act of unenlightened self-negation.

There are deeper questions one can ask concerning the nature, targeting, timing and efficacy of the violence of the CIA-created "jihad" movement. For now we will state only that the idea of any benefit accruing as a result of "Islamic" terror died December 25, 2009 aboard Detroit-bound Northwest Flight 253. Its tombstone is in the Detroit-area dungeon Farouk Abdul Mutallab has been thrown into.

Conclusion

So what is the connection between these disparate ideas buried in Graveyard Detroit? African Americans, most of whom are still waiting for the deposit of the funds for the bad check Dr. King referred to in one of his speeches; the white middle class whose homes, retirement and pension funds, jobs and sense of security have been stolen by the latter-day robber barons; and Muslims along with others whose lives and lands have been or will soon be laid waste by the American war machine must see that they are being brutalized by the same globalized corporate hegemony. That being the case, they must find ways to unite if their resistance to those corporate forces is to have any efficacy or meaning.

African Americans cannot see Latinos who are "stealing all of the jobs" as the enemy. They must understand that the system that forces *campesinos* from their lands through unjust and inequitable agricultural policies and sends them flowing desperately northward, is the same system that criminalizes young African American men and then profits off their incarceration. It is also the same system that is responsible for a 50 percent unemployment rate among black youth and directs more of those youth towards prison than towards a university classroom.

Disenfranchised white folks must understand that Islam is neither their enemy nor a threat to their existence any more than the Vietnamese in the 1960s or Latin Americans leftist organizations in the 1980s. All of our "enemies du jour" are just desperate people trying to the best of their understanding and ability to preserve their land, culture, and resources against the rapacious appetite of a global empire. It is not the Muslims who have closed down their factories, eliminated their jobs, stolen their retirement funds, devalued their homes, and burdened their children with a mountain of debt by bailing out the banks, insurance underwriters and finance houses.

Furthermore, the white middle class has to stop the mindless game of political musical chairs, alternately blaming the incumbent party, be it the Democrats or the Republicans, for the ravages of a pathological system. The problem is not the Democrats or the Republicans; both parties have sold out to the corporate interests whose army of lobbyists floods Capital Hill shelling out money to the political quislings who in turn sell out the voters they pretend so hypocritically to serve. The problem is a system that facilitates such pernicious nonsense.

The mounting frustrations of the white middle class against the failures and excesses of the political system will not be solved by tea party protests or scapegoating hapless groups such as Muslims or Latino immigrants. Only united and focused nonviolent political movement that works to undo the oppressive structures that advance what Dr. Martin Luther King, Jr. referred to as the evil triplets of poverty, racism, and militarism will lead to any lasting change in this country. The white middle class, or its surviving vestiges, must be an integral part of such a movement.

For their part, Muslims must have the wisdom, insight and sagacity to realize that the current wars being visited upon Muslims are not evidence of an American crusade against the faithful, any more than the Vietnam War or the invasions of Panama or Grenada were crusades. They are all geostrategic conflagrations fueled by an outdated Machiavellian logic that ultimately transcends religion.

Muslims must also realize that in some instances impoverished people in America are brutalized by the police, prison guards, ICE officers and other agents of the state in ways that make many poor neighborhoods in America microcosms of occupied Muslim lands.

The validity of this comparison is reinforced by the image of Blackwater mercenaries prowling the streets of New Orleans keeping the "refugees" in check in the aftermath of Hurricane Katrina.

Muslims must also understand that there are many American groups and individuals, including Jewish ones, who are working tirelessly to reverse the policies that demonize Muslims and direct bombs and missiles towards their lands. Furthermore, Muslims must see that only by forming bonds of solidarity with those oppressed groups in America will they gain the critical mass needed to begin addressing their grievances and meaningfully alleviating their suffering.

There is no group that alone can undo the dangerous policies and politics of a global empire that in many ways threatens the very existence of our planet. Opposing that oppressive force will require a globalized resistance that has the ability to replicate monstrous corporations and their surrogates in their ability to transcend national boundaries. That resistance must have the insight to engage in a deep level of analysis that looks beyond the superficial categories presented by corporate-sponsored pundits and ideologues to see the underlying causes of our collective problems, the structures that unite the disparate groups that suffer as a result of the policies that facilitate the corporate dominance of the world, and the strategies that will be needed to move forward.

If Graveyard Detroit can teach us anything, it is the degree to which our lives have become intertwined. Whites, African Americans and large numbers of Arabs, many of them Muslims –Lebanese, Iraqis, Yemenis and others- live in and around Detroit. Globalizing economic forces have brought them together, and despite the periodic traumas and great stresses that threaten to tear them apart they have been able to form a civic community, which had come together to begin to rebuild their city, prior to the 2008 financial meltdown. If these communities are able to regroup and cross the lines of division, perhaps their example will inspire a world in desperate need for new direction; Graveyard Detroit can become a place of resurrection.

4.

I AM MY SISTER'S KEEPER

In the literature discussing *futuwwa*, which has been translated as Muslim chivalry, there is the story of a young man who was engaged to marry a particularly beautiful woman. Before the wedding day, his fiancée was afflicted with a severe case of chicken pox, which left her face terribly disfigured. Her father wrote to inform him of the situation and asked if he preferred to call off the wedding. The young man replied stating that he would still marry his daughter, but that he had recently experienced a gradual loss of sight, which he feared would culminate in blindness.

The wedding proceeded as planned and the couple had a loving and happy relationship until the wife died twenty years later. Upon her death the husband regained his eyesight. When asked about his seemingly miraculous recovery he explained that he could see all along. He had feigned blindness all those years because he did not want to offend or sadden his wife.

From our jaded or cynical vantage points it is easy to dismiss such a story as a preposterous fabrication. To do so is to miss an important point that was not lost to those who circulated and were inspired by this and similar tales. Namely, our religion is not an empty compilation of laws and strictures. The law is important and willingly accepting it is one of the keys to our salvation. However, the law is also a means that points us towards a higher ethical end. We are reminded in the Qur'an, "Surely, the prayer wards off indecency and lewdness"(29:45).

The Prophet, peace and blessings upon him, mentioned concerning the fast, "One who does not abandon false speech and acting on its imperatives, God has no need that he gives up his food and drink" (Bukhari, 1903). These narrations emphasize that there is far more to Islam than a mere adherence to rulings.

This is especially true in our marriages. Too many Muslims are involved in marriages that devolve into an empty observation of duties and an equally vacuous demand for the fulfillment of rights. While such practices are laudable in their proper context, when they are divorced from kindness, consideration, empathy, and true commitment they define marriages that become a fragile caricature. Such relationships are irreparably shattered by a silly argument, a few wrinkles on the face, unwanted pounds around the waist, a personality quirk or a desire to play the field to see if one can latch on to someone prettier, wealthier, younger, or possibly more exciting than one's spouse.

These are issues that affect both men and women. However, we men must step up and do our part to help to arrest the alarmingly negative state of gender relations in our communities. The level of chivalry the current crisis demands does not require that we pretend to be blind or have poor vision for twenty years. However, it does require some serious soul searching, and it demands that we ask ourselves some hard questions. Below are a few areas where our inquiries might begin.

Why are so many Muslim men averse to marrying older or previously married women? The general feeling among the women folk in our communities is that if you are not married by the age of twenty-five, then you have only two chances of being married thereafter –slim and none. This sentiment pervades our sisters' minds and hearts because of the reality they experience. Many brothers who put off marriage until they are past thirty-five will oftentimes marry someone close to half their age, passing over a generation of women who are intellectually and psychologically more compatible with them and would prove wiser parents for their children.

Despite this problem, and the clear social, psychological and cultural pathologies it breeds, many of us will hasten to give a lecture reminding our audience of the fact that Khadija, the beloved wife of our Prophet, peace upon him, was fifteen years his senior. We might even mention that she and several of his other wives were previously married. Why is it that what was good enough for our Prophet, peace upon him, is repugnant to our sons or ourselves?

A related question would be, "Why are so many of our brothers so hesitant to marry strong, independent and intellectually astute women?" Many women in the West lack the support of extended family networks, which is increasingly true even in the Muslim world. Therefore, they must seek higher education or professional training to be in a position to support themselves, if necessary, or assist their husbands, an increasingly likely scenario owing to the nature of work in postindustrial societies. Others, having received the same education as men, see themselves as possessing the same career choices and opportunities as their male counterparts. These sociological facts leads to women in the West generally manifesting a degree of education and independence that might not be present among women in more traditional societies –even though such societies are rapidly disappearing.

Many Muslim men will pass over talented, educated women who are willing to put their careers and education on hold, if need be, to commit to a family. The common reason given is that such women are too assertive, or they are not the kind of women the prospective husband's mother prefers. As a result a significant number of our sisters, despite their beauty, talent, maturity, and dynamism are passed over for marriage in favor of an idealized, demure "real" Muslim woman. The social consequences of this practice are extremely grave for our community.

Again, we can ask ourselves, "To what extent does this practice conform to the prophetic model?" Our Prophet was surrounded by strong, assertive and independent women. His beloved Khadija, who we have previously mentioned, was one of the most successful business people in the Arabian Peninsula, and her wealth allowed the Prophet to retreat to the Cave of Hira where he would receive the first revelation. Aisha, despite her young age was an aggressive, free-spirited, intellectual powerhouse who would become one of the great female scholars in history. The foundation for her intellectual greatness was laid by the Prophet himself, who recognized her brilliance. Zainab bint Jahsh ran a non-profit organization. She would make various handicrafts, sell them in the market and then use the proceeds to secretly give charity to the poor people of Madina. Umm Salama, had the courage to migrate from Mecca to Medina, unescorted, although she was ultimately accompanied by a single rider. She also had the vision to resolve the crisis at Hudaybiyya. These were all wives of the Prophet, peace upon him. To their names we could add those of many other strong and dynamic women who played a major role in the life of the fledgling Muslim community.

Another issue that is leading to many otherwise eligible women remaining single relates to color. If a panel of Muslim men, whose origins were in the Muslim world, were to choose Miss World, the title would likely never leave Scandinavia. No matter how beautiful a woman with a brown, black, or even tan complexion was, she would never be quite beautiful enough because of her skin color. This attitude informs the way many choose their wives. This is a sensitive issue, but it is one we must address if we are to advance as a community. We may think that ours is a "colorblind" community; however, there are legions of women who have been relegated to the status of unmarriageable social pariahs who would beg to differ.

God has stated that the basis for virtue with Him is piety, not tribe, race, or national origin (49:13). The Prophet, peace upon him, reminded us that God does not look at our physical forms, or at our wealth. Rather, He looks at our hearts and our deeds (Muslim, 2564). We debase ourselves when we exalt what God has belittled. God and his Messenger, peace upon him, have belittled skin color as a designator of virtue or distinction. What does it say about us when we use it as a truncheon to painfully bludgeon some of the most beautiful women imaginable into social insignificance?

Marriage is not a playground where the ego thoughtlessly pursues its vanities. This is something the chivalrous young man mentioned at the outset of this essay understood. It is an institution that helps a man and a woman pursue the purpose of their creation: to glorify and worship God and to work, within the extent of our capabilities and resources, to make the world a better place for those we share it with and for those we will leave it to. This role is beautifully captured in the Qur'an, "The believing men and women are each other's supporting friends. They enjoin right, forbid wrong, establish regular prayer, pay the poor due, and they obey God and His Messenger. They expect God's Mercy. Surely, God is Mighty, Wise (9:71)."

5.

THOMAS FRIEDMAN:
PRISONER IN A GLASS HOUSE

Thomas Friedman, in his New York Times Op-ed entitled, "www.jihad.com," claims that Muslims lack the moral courage to condemn the murderous outrages of "Jihadi" extremists in their midst. Part of the reason for this moral failure, in his view, is because the West has not demanded that Muslims take responsibility for their societies, beginning with a strong condemnation of the extremists amongst them. Friedman states that without such a condemnation, coupled with concerted action, America's efforts to rebuild the Muslim world in her image will prove a futile endeavor.

Friedman posits that very few Muslim political or religious leaders are willing to challenge the violent ideology of Islamic extremists. However, Friedman apparently fails to realize is that there is an intense ideological struggle underway in the Muslim world and at the heart of that struggle is the effort of orthodox scholars to delegitimize the arguments of those who would use Islamic teachings to justify wanton violence and destruction. Furthermore, contrary to his assessment, orthodoxy is gaining the upper hand.

In making his argument, Friedman quotes Mamoun Fandy, an analyst at London's Institute of Strategic Studies, as saying: "What Muslims were talking about last week were the minarets of Switzerland, not the killings of people in Iraq or Pakistan." Indeed, there are Muslims who are concerned about the fate of their coreligionists in the West, and are quick to comment on the real or perceived injustices involving Muslims in western lands. However, most of those commentators also condemn the violence of the modern-day *Khawarij*[14] with far more words, passion and fervor.

By way of example, Shaykh Abdullah bin Bayyah, one of the preeminent jurists in the Muslim world, has written a brief statement on the Swiss minaret controversy. However, he has recently written an entire book condemning the violence and misinterpretations of the so-called "Jihadis." That book is currently being translated into English and will be available in this country early next year.

Shaykh bin Bayyah is not alone. Many scholars from al-Azhar University, the most prestigious center of learning in the Muslim world, have been engaging in a deep dialogue with members of *al-Gama'ah al-Islamiyya, Jihad Islami* and other violent Egyptian groups. This dialogue has led to hundreds, if not thousands, of members of these groups renouncing violence against civilian and noncombatant forces. It has resulted in thousands of pages of literature and passionate societal discussion in Egypt. Dr. Sherman Jackson, an Islamic studies and Arabic professor at the University of Michigan is currently translating some of this literature into English and has lectured extensively about this initiative.

A similar effort by scholars and jurists in Yemen has also met with tremendous success. Even within the Jihad movement, there is intense debate about the moral sanction and strategic efficacy of violence against civilian and noncombatant targets. An excellent article, *The Rebellion Within*, which examines this issue in great detail, appeared in the June 2, 2008 edition of the New Yorker Magazine. Written by Lawrence Wright, the article highlighted one of the most influential theorists of the Jihad movement, Dr. Fadl, born Sayyid Imam al-Sharif, and his rejection of the wanton violence of al-Qaeda.

This critical debate about the moral validity and strategic efficacy of violence is raging in every Muslim society. Even in Palestine, many have questioned the moral, strategic, and tactical efficacy of suicide bombings against Israeli targets. The current cessation of that tactic there indicates that the voices arguing against it are prevailing. One wonders how Friedman can completely disregard all of these developments as he condesendingly tells "infantilized" Muslims what they must do to put their house in order.

Friedman is free to condemn Muslims for a lack of moral courage. However, the same issue he raises can be posed to American political and religious leaders. Namely, when will they find the moral courage to seriously challenge the American war machine that is currently spending a trillion dollars a year, more than the rest of the world combined, for war? If Friedman thinks that the violence visited upon Muslims by America is less a factor in stimulating Muslims to contemplate violent actions than the agitation of al-Qaeda or similar movements, he is seriously mistaken.

I ask Friedman, are not Americans just as "objectified" in their passive acquiescence to what President Dwight Eisenhower referred to as the "military industrial complex," and the tremendous violence ensuing from it, as are Muslims, according to his view? Friedman argues that Islam needs a civil war to confront the odious ideology of a violent minority that believes it is acceptable to murder both Muslims and non-Muslims who will not accept "the most rigid Muslim lifestyle and submit to rule by a Muslim caliphate." By this reasoning, must America wage another civil war to challenge the foul idea that any country that will not submit to American strategic designs should be bombed, invaded, occupied, or otherwise systematically destroyed?

Americans defeated the idea of slavery domestically. However, have we as a society defeated that idea internationally? What is the fate of those weak people and states that will not submit to our political and economic domination? Are they not brutalized and punished in the most horrific fashion –just as rebellious slaves are?

As Friedman argues, a corrosive mindset has indeed set in since 9/11. That corrosion is not limited to what he mentions. That corrosive mindset also posits that hapless Muslims are the major cause of violence and instability in the world and to deal with them we must engage in preemptive wars, develop a generation of tactical nuclear weapons to use exclusively against them, bomb, invade and occupy their lands on the flimsiest pretexts and then remain silent as they are demonized and dehumanized in the media.

I make Friedman a wager. I bet that Muslims will wage an ideological civil war to address their violent extremists long before Americans will wage one to address ours. I venture that long after Muslims have reclaimed their subjectivity in this regard, most "objectified" Americans will still passively acquiesce to the inhuman imperatives of the military, and now, terror industrial complexes. Time will tell who will win.

6.

THE DEEPER IMPLICATIONS OF MUSLIMS TARGETING CIVILIANS

This essay, written in the immediate aftermath of the failed New York City bomb attempt, will examine some of the theological implications of Muslims violating civilian immunity. I have previously written why attacks against innocent civilians are in opposition to fundamental teachings of Islam. Unfortunately, there are some Muslim ideologues that sanction such actions of their coreligionists who have killed an increasing number of Muslim civilians and noncombatants in Iraq, Afghanistan[15] and elsewhere. For these reasons, the argument that follows is more than merely hypothetical.

Western military commanders, politicians and philosophers who have sanctioned the widespread bombing of civilian populations –owing to the industrialization of war and its being wedded with nationalist ideology during the 19th and 20th centuries- realize that their actions involve a dangerous moral leap. The following passage from Phillip Meilinger's work on the moral implications of modern warfare illustrates this point:

> The Fall of France in 1940 left Britain alone against Germany. The ensuing Battle of Britain, culminating in the Blitz, left England reeling. Surrender was unthinkable, but it could not retaliate with its outnumbered and overstretched army and navy. The only hope of hitting back at Germany and winning the war lay with Bomber Command. But operational factors quickly demonstrated that prewar factors [emphasizing precision bombing of military objectives] had been hopelessly unrealistic. ...Aircrew survival dictated night area attacks, and, in truth, there was little alternative other than not to attack at all. Moral constraints bowed to what was deemed military necessity, which led air leaders down a particularly slippery slope.[16]

That slippery slope led to massacres of civilians that were unprecedented in history and culminated in the nuclear incineration of the Japanese cities of Hiroshima and Nagasaki. Muslims who would sanction gross violations of civilian immunity, owing to strategic desperation, are entering on a similarly slippery slope. However, there is a huge difference between the norms that govern Western strategic thinking and those defined by Islam. Namely, Western norms are socially constructed while those defined by Islam have their origin in revelation –the latter as understood by Muslims. Hence, from a Muslim perspective, and that perspective is critical for the argument we are making, Western norms are subject to change with changes in social, political, economic and especially technological considerations, while Islamic norms are transcendent.[17]

The idea of total war, which holds that there is no distinction between the combatant and noncombatant elements of an enemy population, and that both groups can legitimately be targeted by an armed force, is ancient. The Peloponnesian War (431-404 BC), as documented by Thucydides, involved both the mobilization of entire populations for the war effort and likewise the eradication of entire populations, such as the inhabitants of Milos. During the Middle Ages, the Mongol invasion of the Muslim heartland of Asia could be described as a campaign of total warfare that left unimaginable death and destruction in its wake.

The existence of total war campaigns during early historical periods is accompanied by efforts to extend immunity from violent conflict to civilians. Plato, various Roman philosophers, Medieval Christian theologians, orders of knights and in the early modern period, theorists such as Francisco de Victoria and Hugo Grotius all advocated various degrees of civilian immunity from the scourges of war.

In the Western intellectual tradition, the thinking surrounding this idea during various historical epochs was associated with prevailing views of just and unjust actions as well as the self-interest of relevant societal actors, as opposed to clear and deeply rooted scriptural pronouncements. This was true even among Christians. Hence, we do not see meaningful discussions on limiting the destructiveness of war among Christian theologians until the 4th Christian Century with the work of St. Augustine.

In Europe, changing conditions and circumstances have led to changing positions on the issue of civilian immunity. For much of the latter Middle Age the prevailing European views were dominated by ideas emerging from the Catholic Church's Peace of God movement, and the writings of St. Thomas Aquinas. The advent of the nation-state in the aftermath of the Peace of Westphalia in 1648 would introduce a new epistemology to govern thinking around strategic affairs, even though Medieval Christian thinking still informed attitudes and policies related to civilian immunity, at least until the French and Industrial Revolutions.

These nearly simultaneous developments led to the idea that the civilian infrastructure needed to support a modern war effort was so essential to its successful prosecution that it transformed civilians into combatants. As a result, beginning with the Napoleonic Wars and the

American Civil War, conflicts in the West would witness the erosion of civilian immunity –at least until the aftermath of World War II.

Unlike the situation prevailing in non-Muslim lands, the idea of civilian immunity among Muslims has been rooted in clear scriptural pronouncements from the prophetic epoch. Qur'anic passages establishing the sanctity of innocent life (5:32) and not expanding hostilities to noncombatants (2:190) coupled with prophetic strictures against killing women, children, monks, and other noncombatants created the basis for a strong and enduring Muslim ethic governing civilian immunity. Although there have clearly been instances when some Muslim rulers and commanders have not respected that ethic, it has generally remained a restraining factor throughout Muslim history.[18]

Among the greatest fruits of this ethical code has been the existence of large non-Muslim populations in historical Muslim empires, the general lack of forced conversion of these non-Muslim communities, and a lack of genocidal massacres undertaken by Muslim armies.[19] It is also evident in the peaceful coexistence of Muslims and other faith communities in areas such as Andalusia, Bosnia, Palestine and Iraq, historically.

As changing geopolitical and technological realities dictate changes in the norms governing the intentional targeting of civilians in Western strategic thinking, there is no inherent damage to the integrity of Western secular thought. Indeed, the socially constructed nature of those norms only serves to reinforce the secularity of the process whereby they are arrived at and the analytical methods governing their assessment. This is not the case for the transcendental Islamic ideal governing civilian immunity. When it is abandoned by Muslims, a critical aspect of the religion itself is abandoned.

As Dr. Tim Winter (Abdul Hakim Murad),[20] expanding the work of John Gray[21] and others, argues, when that abandonment occurs in the modern context, it is precisely because the transcendental Islamic ideal has been forsaken or lost. Those Muslims who target civilians are robbed of any moral high ground in their struggle with opposing forces and are left vulnerable before the bitter winds of political expediency. In the view of those who have entered upon this vile path, if expediency demands suicidal murder, bombs in mosques and marketplaces or in the heart of Western cities, then so be it.

At the heart of the Islamic ethic regarding the sanctity of innocent life is the following verse in the Qur'an, alluded to earlier:

> Owing to that [first instance murder] we ordained for the Children of Israel that whosoever takes an innocent life for other than retribution for murder or murderous sedition in the land it is as if he has killed all of humanity, and whoever saves a life it is as if he has saved all of humanity. Our Messengers have come to them with clear proofs, yet even after that many of them exceed limits in the land[22] (5:32).

من أجل ذلك كتبنا على بني إسرائيل أنه من قتل نفسا بغير نفس أو فساد في الأرض فكأنما قتل الناس جميعا و من أحياها فكأنما أحيا الناس جميعا و لقد جاءتهم رسلنا بالبينات ثم إن كثيرا منهم بعد ذلك في الأرض لمسرفون

This verse emphasizes that the immunity extended to innocents is a principle that was upheld by all of the Prophets. Hence, the specific mention of the Children of Israel, who were the recipients of a long line of Prophets, and the mentioning of the Messengers at the end of the verse.

The idea that to discard the immunity that is extended to innocents is to abandon an indispensible aspect of the divine law is emphasized by Imam al-Qurtubi in his commentary on this verse (5:32). He states:

> The meaning is that whoever makes it lawful to take the life of a single innocent person has made everyone's life lawful, because he has rejected the divine law [establishing the prohibition of killing innocents].[23]

المعنى أن من استحل واحدا فقد استحل الجميع لأنه أنكر الشرع

Abandoning the divine law when one makes the blood of innocent people lawful to shed is emphasized from a deeper perspective by Imam Fakruddin al-Razi in his commentary on the same verse. He states:

> When he [a murderer] resolves to intentionally kill an innocent person he has given preference to the dictates of his bloodlust and anger over the dictates of obeying God. When this prioritization occurs, in his heart he has resolved to kill anyone who opposes his demands, were he capable of doing so.[24]

أنه لما أقدم على القتل العمد العدوان فقد رجح داعية الشهوة و الغضب على داعية الطاعة و متى كان الأمر كذلك كان هذا الترجيح حاصلا بالنسبة إلى كل واحد فكان في قلبه أن كل أحد نازعه من مطالبه فإنه لو قدر عليه لقتله

The murderous campaigns undertaken by some misguided Muslims that have led to the massacre of thousands of civilians in the Muslim world and that are now threatening innocent people in this country are not manifestations of jihad, as some claim. Rather, they are a mirror image of the godless murderous mayhem and carnage this country has inflicted on the innocent civilians of many Muslim countries, and, as explained above, it involves an abandonment of the prophetic legacy.

Every Muslim who is concerned for the future of his or her faith and the future of the prophetic legacy in the world is morally obliged to work in whatever capacity he or she can to stop attacks that target innocent civilians by any party —Muslims or members of other communities. The basis for this moral obligation is powerfully stated by Imam Razi in his commentary on (5:32). He mentions:

> If all of humanity knew that a single individual intends to exterminate them they would undoubtedly try their utmost to prevent him from obtaining his objective. Likewise, if they knew that he intends to kill a single person then their seriousness and exertion in trying to deter him from killing

that person should be just as great as it would be in preventing their own mass murder.[25]

هو أن جميع الناس لو علموا أنه يقصد قتلهم بأجمعهم فلا شك أنهم يدفعونه دفعا لا يمكنه تحصيل مقصوده
فكذلك إذا علموا منه أنه يقصد قتل إنسان واحد معين يجب أن يكون جدهم واجتهادهم في منعه عن قتل ذلك الإنسان مثل جدهم
واجتهادهم في الصورة الأولى

The reason for this is that the life of a single innocent person has
the sanctity of the lives of all humanity. This is an ideal we cannot let
die. If we allow it to die who will revive it? Human history has shown
how quickly we can begin a free fall into murderous madness once we
have entered upon the path that justifies murdering innocent civilians
and other noncombatants. If the American military and the warmongering interests supporting it are guilty in this regard we condemn
them in the strongest terms, and if our fellow Muslims are guilty we
must likewise, condemn them.

The only difference between the two cases is that when the
American military kills innocent civilians it is violating principles of
human rights and worldly conventions, which, as we have seen with
the current arguments justifying torture, are subject to change or being
discarded altogether. When Muslims do it, we are betraying our faith
and the legacy of the Prophets, peace upon them, who have left us
a wealth of timeless, enduring wisdom.

7.

RALLYING OF THE MUHAMMADAIC FORCES

I recently attended two major Muslim conferences where Christian fundamentalists were "protesting" against a Muslim presence in "Christian" America. In each instance, the demonstrators were shabbily clad, apparently from the poorer elements of American society. Their faces were red with anger and their violent voices exuded rage. They stood in sharp contrast to the beautiful, dignified, modestly dressed and peaceful Muslims they were directing their scorn towards.

The scene was deeply ironic. Here was a group of Christians, whose very presence spoke of an irrational detestation void of any compassion or empathy, telling an assembly of Muslims, whose cheerful countenances and stately comportment expressed human refinement, that their religion was one of hatred and violence. In any case, they must have realized how ridiculous they appeared, for they soon packed up and left.

It is possible that this was the first time any of these folks had actually seen Muslims in person. The caricaturized images of the Muslim "terrorist" so prevalent in various media likely informed their idea of what a Muslim is and motivated their protests. However, the reality of the Muslims they actually encountered was a powerful corrective to those images and likely created a severe psychological conflict, which they could not easily reconcile.

The encounter was one of truth and falsehood. Truth prevailed. We should realize that whenever truth encounters falsehood, truth will always prevail. God mentions in the Qur'an, "Truth arrives and falsehood perishes; falsehood is inherently perishable" (17:81). Similarly, "Rather, We hurl the truth at falsehood and it renders it unintelligible" (21:18).

Now is not the time for Muslims in the West to hide or run away in the face of the abuses some elements in Western societies are directing towards Islam and its adherents. Now is the time for us to stand up and become messengers and ambassadors of the truth we profess. This is the only way we will defeat the lies, distortions, and propaganda that have made even some Muslims question the possibility of a positive future for Muslims in the Western world.

The greatest truth we possess is not that articulated by our words. When so much negativity is associated with Islam in Western lands, at a certain point, to paraphrase a popular American idiom, "Talk is cheap." Many people, who do not know ordinary Muslims, have an impression of Islam that has been shaped by images of screaming mobs, hooded assassins and stories of unspeakable atrocities. For these folks, words alone cannot displace the images that have been etched in their consciousness, and do little to dispel their fear.

Such images can only be replaced by an alternative image; one whose power is rooted in the fertile soil of devotion and whose strength is forged in the timeless furnace of humility. Those images first enter the heart, before they endeavor to address the mind, and they are conveyed by the gentle breezes of mercy and service. Those alternative images may also involve words. However, those words are spoken by the tongue of the spiritual state, and they spring forth from the heart, not the mouth.

Oftentimes, we may read passages such as the above and take them to be the empty ramblings of weaklings who dare not confront the rapacious force of Western imperialism and militarism with the strength of our own Muslim arms. Such passages are seen by some as the escapist path of those who fear embracing the Qur'anic declaration, "Fight in the Way of God those who fight you…" (2:190).

However, those who cannot see beyond this physical world have in many instances bitten into the poisonous fruit of material power. As a result, Qur'anic truths, which alert them to sources of metaphysical strength, become marginalized in both their consciousness and in their strategic thinking. They cannot see the power and strategic import of the verse, "Good and evil are not equal. Respond [to evil] with what is better. Unexpectedly, the one between who you and he there was enmity becomes like an intimate friend." They cannot understand the great power embodied in prophetic truths such as the saying of the Messenger of God, peace and blessings upon him, "…God renders mighty a servant who can pardon others, and He exalts anyone who can humble himself for His Sake (Muslim, 2588)."

Veiled from seeing the reality of the metaphysical world that gives meaning and efficacy to these sort of passages, they become so obsessed with a reliance on their meager human resources, and so oblivious to the boundless power of God, that they delusionally believe they can augment their strength in ways that may in reality turn the power of God against them. Murder, suicide, mayhem and terror become their means for seeking God's help, as opposed to patience and prayer. When they do not receive divine aid, they begin to envision ever more desperate means towards the attainment of their ends. Machiavelli may be smiling in his grave, but not Muhammad, peace and blessings upon him.

It is time for the souls who have imbibed the fragrance of the truth brought by Muhammad, peace upon him, whose live-giving aroma is currently effusing the world, to rise. Their uprising will not be one of angry mobs demanding justice at any cost even that purchased with the currency of vengeance so bitter that it disguises the hubris of its advocates. If that is the state of the mob, perhaps Nemesis will be confused and descend upon that mob even though it is nominally advocating justice.

The uprising of righteous souls will not be that of frenzied mobs descending into the streets. It will be the rising up of committed believers from the sweetness of sleep in the privacy of their homes, to stand before their Lord in deep devotion. That uprising will not begin during the day, nor will it be played out before flashing lights and cameras. It will begin during the night before the watchful gaze of God.

The feet of its soldiers will not be clad in boots smashing against pavement. Their feet will be bare, caressing carpets, straw mats or clammy cement, supporting hearts tearfully beseeching their Lord, evoking His Grace, seeking His Succor, acknowledging their faults and limitations and seeking their strength through Him.

When they emerge into the light of day they themselves will be the light that a dark world is seeking. They will be teachers not preachers. Their message will be ancient for it will be a rearticulating of the prophetic teachings –as reiterated in the Qur'an:

- Do not join partners with God in worship for doing so is an unforgiveable sin (4:48)

- Make God the ultimate object of your love, for doing so is a sign of true faith (2:165, 9:24)

- Do not commit murder or take innocent lives, for doing so is a crime that has unfathomable implications (25:68, 17:33)

- Uphold the dignity of all humans, for it is a gift from God (17:70)

- Work against corrupt, unethical business practices for they are condemned by God (26:181-183, 83:1-3)

- Feed the hungry for it wards off Hell and is a manifestation of lofty religiousness (74:44, 90:14-16)

- Assist the needy, for they have a right in our wealth (51:19, 70:24-25)

- Be loving and merciful to your spouse for it is a Sign of God (30:21)

- Do not oppress anyone, for God hates oppressors (3:57, 3:140, 42:40)

- Do not fornicate for it is a grave abomination and a source of a severe otherworldly punishment (25:68)

- Do not corrupt the earth and disrupt the natural balance governing worldly ecosystems for doing so brings about devastating consequences (33:41, 55:6-15)

- In all things follow the example of the Noble Prophet for it is a key to salvation (33:21)

- If tested with warfare do not violate the rules of engagement established by God, for victory only comes from God, not from lowly, treacherous tactics. (2:177, 3:126)

These forces will bring life to morally and spiritually dead societies for they themselves have been revivified by the life-giving message of Islam: "O Believers! Respond to God and the Messenger when they invite you to what gives life" (8:24). Their existence will be defined by purpose as they strive to embody the message of faith translated in lives of devotion. The lives and souls of others they touch will be quickened by those same realities.

This is the basis of the good life and the foundation of a community of virtue and service. This is the foundation of meaningful and lasting social reform. It is on this basis that we can hope for the emergence of a community of truth whose light cannot be hidden or diminished by any amount of distortion and defamation. Let each and every one of us commit ourselves to being part of that community. God is calling us and history is echoing His call. Who among us is prepared to respond?

8.

LIVING THE QUR'AN

During Ramadan we celebrate the Qur'an. This is fitting owing to the close association between the month of fasting and the Qur'an. Allah mentions in the Qur'an, "The month of Ramadan in which the Qur'an was revealed" (Q. 2: 185). This association is connected to the fact that during the month we recite the sacred scripture as often as we can.

Reciting the Qur'an is a highly rewarded act of worship. The Prophet, peace and blessings of God upon him, mentioned in this regard, "Whoever recites a single letter from the Qur'an will have a reward, and that reward will be multiplied tenfold. Do not say that "Alif-Lam-Mim" is a single letter. Rather, "Alif" is a distinct letter, "Lam" is a distinct letter, and "Mim" is a distinct letter."[26] One cannot begin to imagine the reward of a believer who recites the entire Qur'an in its entirety once, twice or thrice during the month of Ramadan.

The scholars of the early generations used to cease their other intellectual pursuits during Ramadan and devote themselves exclusively to the Qur'an. It is related that 'Umar would instruct Ubayy bin Ka'b and Tamim al-Dari to lead the people in prayer during this blessed month. They would recite up to two hundred verses in a single unit of prayer (rakat), until some of the congregation would lean on canes for support owing to the length of the recitation, but even so they would not disperse until just before Fajr.[27] Some of the earlier generations of Muslims would complete the Qur'an every third night in Ramadan, others in seven, yet others in ten.[28]

Ibn Rajab further relates:

> The early Muslims would recite the Qur'an during prayer and at other times during Ramadan. Al-Aswad used to complete the Qur'an every other night during Ramadan. Al-Nakha'i would read at that rate during the last ten days specifically. During the balance of the month he would complete it every third night. Qatada would complete the Qur'an every seven days throughout the year, but during Ramadan every third night. During the last ten days of the month he would complete it every night. During Ramadan Imam Shafi'i would complete the Qur'an sixty times, all of them outside of prayer. Abu Hanifa would read at a similar pace. [...] Ibn 'Abd al-Hakam relates that when Ramadan began Imam Malik would turn away from teaching Hadith, scholarly circles and devote himself to reciting the Qur'an from the *Mushaf*. 'Abd al-Razzaq mentioned that Sufyan al-Thawri would leave off all other [non-obligatory] devotional acts during Ramadan and concentrate on reciting the Qur'an. 'Aisha, may Allah be pleased with her, would recite the Qur'an during the latter part of the night during Ramadan and not sleep until after the rising of the sun. When Ramadan started Zubayd al-Yami would bring out the Qur'ans and gather his associates together to recite them.[29]

He adds:

> Rather, the prohibition against completing the Qur'an in less than three days is against doing that constantly. As for exceptionally virtuous times such as the Month of Ramadan, especially the days during which the Night of Decrees (Layla al-Qadr) is sought out; or in especially virtuous places, such as Mecca, for those who are not permanent residents there, it is highly desirable to increase the rate of recitation to take advantage of the [blessed nature] of the time and place.[30]

We relate these passages to give the reader a sense of the devotion those early generations had to the Qur'an—and those who have followed their example throughout the long generations during which the saga of Islam has unfolded on the earth.

They not only recited the Qur'an, they also studied it, served it, acted on its commandments and prohibitions and lived lives informed by the worldview that it presented. Part of their service to the Qur'an was their preservation of the Arabic language through the development of the various linguistic sciences of grammar, morphology, syntax, rhetoric, phonology, etymology, semantics and monumental works of lexicography. The work of the early Muslims in these areas stands as one of the greatest intellectual enterprises in human history.

Hence, the Qur'an was a source of their strength and they were elevated by it. The Prophet, peace and blessings upon him, stated, "God elevates by means of this Book (The Qur'an) nations and He debases others."[31] The early generations of this community were not elevated by the Qur'an in terms of worldly power and influence alone; they were a spiritually enlightened community exemplified by exalted manners and noble characteristics.

The Qur'an can also be the source of our elevation. I have seen a glimpse of that in myself. During my first term as the imam of Masjid al-Islam in New Haven, Connecticut from 1987 to 1994, the community was committed to the Qur'an. During Ramadan we would do two complete readings of the Qur'an as a community, one during the special Ramadan prayers (Tarawih) and one during the late night prayers during the last ten days of the month. Families would bring their infant children to sleep in a room adjoining the prayer area during the service.

We would complete the Qur'an in a circle after morning prayer on a regular basis. Young men, some of whom were struggling in school, would join the circle and learn to recite the Qur'an in Arabic in two to three weeks. We would seek out the meanings and endeavor to understand and implement the commandments presented by the Book. As a result, the community was strong and cohesive. There is no denying that we had the same social ills present in other inner-city communities, but compared to others places they were minimal.

As we survey the current Muslim landscape we see in many places a gloomy picture. Divorces and other indices of social dysfunction are skyrocketing. Many individuals are struggling with faith crises. If we look at the connection to the Qur'an, both at a communal and an individual level, we see a highly undesirable situation in which the Qur'an has largely been abandoned. God mentions in the Qur'an, "The Messenger (Muhammad) said, 'O My Lord! My people have treated this Qur'an as [something lowly], easily forsaken' (25:30). This revelation immediately refers to the Quraysh, the Prophet's tribe, and their contemptible rejection of the Qur'an. However, at another level, we are also his people and part of his complaint to God, in this regard, may be relevant for many of us.

Unlike the Quraysh, we believe in the Qur'an. However, like them we can fail to listen to it or recite it, we can fail to act on its message and meanings, and we can forsake it until it has no influence on our daily lives. These are all things we should strenuously endeavor to avoid. One of the ways to avoid these things is to realize the transformative power of the Qur'an and then to actively invite that power into our lives.

The Qur'an, when it is a regular part of our lives, connects us to a community of meaning. That community then manifests certain lofty ethics and exalted morals. This is so because words and language have a deeply defining and transformative power. Consider this quote from Neil Postman:

> If we define ideology as a set of assumptions of which we are barely conscious but which nonetheless directs our efforts to give shape and coherence to the world, then our most powerful ideological instrument is the technology of language itself. Language is pure ideology. It instructs us not only in the names of things but, more important, in what things can be named. It divides the world into subjects and objects. It denotes what events shall be regarded as processes, and what events, things. It instructs us about time, space, and number, and forms our ideas of how we stand in relation to nature and to each other. In English grammar, for example, there are always subjects who act, and verbs which are their actions, and objects which are acted upon. It is a rather aggressive grammar, which makes it difficult for those of us who must use it to think of the world as benign.
>
> Of course, most of us, most of the time, are unaware of how language does its work. We live deep within the boundaries of our linguistic assumptions and have little sense of how the world looks to those who speak a vastly different tongue. We tend to assume that everyone sees the world in the same way, irrespective of differences in language. Only occasionally is this illusion challenged, as when the differences between linguistic ideologies become noticeable by one who has command of two languages that differ greatly in their structure and history.[32]

The linguistic assumptions along with the denotative and connotative power of Arabic in general and Qur'anic Arabic specifically, create a universe of meaning that give shape to a tangible historical community that transcends race, ethnicity, geographical barriers and time. However, to become part of that community, one has to be connected to the Qur'an. Otherwise, although one will remain Muslim, the transformative power of Islam will not be at work to the fullest extent in one's life.[33]

This reality of Qur'anic Arabic as a transformative power has been brilliantly described by Toshihiko Izutsu in his notable study, *Ethico-Religious Concepts in the Qur'an*.[34] Izutsu summarizes that power in the following paragraph:

> The whole matter is based on the fundamental idea that each linguistic system –Arabic is one, and Qur'anic Arabic is another- represents a group of coordinated concepts which, together, reflect a particular *Weltanschauung*, commonly shared by, and peculiar to, the speakers of the language in question. Thus Qur'anic Arabic corresponds, in its connotative aspect, to what we may rightly call the Qur'anic world-view, which in itself is simply a segment of that wider world-view mirrored by the classical Arabic language. In exactly the same way, the ethical language of the Qur'an represents only a segment of the whole Qur'anic world-view. And the ethico-religious terms constitute a small, relatively independent, system within that ethical segment.[35]

As Izutsu's study illustrates, the Qur'anic worldview became the basis for a moral and ethical transformation of the Arabs. That Qur'anic transformation was not disconnected from the pre-Qur'anic classical Arabic language. Rather it was rooted in it. However, it was nonetheless deeply transformative in and of itself.

If the Qur'an is to effect a similar transformation in our community we must get in touch with the Qur'an. To do this, we must recite it, study it, endeavor to learn its language and above all, live it. To effectively begin that process, we are required to make some fundamental changes in how we spend our time and the linguistic influences we expose ourselves to.

Currently, the average Muslim is inundated with mostly English language messages that are rooted in a worldview reflecting the imperatives of power, control, domination, individualism and material consumption. Most of those messages reach us through television and the internet. If we are to avoid being shaped by that worldview we will have to greatly limit our exposure to those messages.

If we are caught up in the cultural currents that are constantly urging greater involvement with this media and their messages, those messages will not only continue to define us, they will rob us of the time needed to begin and sustain the process of Qur'anic transformation. We will need to institute anti-television initiatives for our communities, schools and families. Additionally, it is imperative that we take measures to ensure that we limit the time we spend engaged with most aspects of the internet, as communities and as individuals.

Finally, as we go about developing such initiatives and encouraging such practices, we must support each other in our quest to make the Qur'an the springtime of our hearts. This requires teaching every member of our communities to recite the Qur'an, even if it is a struggle for some people and we must encourage the study of the Arabic language. We must emphasize the great reward they will receive for their struggle and exertion. To make this a reality, we must institute study circles in our communities where we gather to study the message of the Qur'an in the language we find ourselves most conversant in.

Most importantly, we must all make a personal commitment to living the Qur'an. Here we are not left without a great source of prophetic guidance, for in the words of 'Aisha, may Allah be pleased with her, "His (The Prophet's) character was an embodiment of the Qur'an."[36] He, peace upon him, is our exemplar; let us follow his way, beginning during this blessed month of the Qur'an.

9.

WE ARE ALL IN THIS TOGETHER

One of the assumptions underlying the current campaign to demonize, criminalize, and delegitimize Muslims as citizens of the United
States, is that of Muslim silence. The orchestrators of that campaign
of demonization, and it is indeed being carefully and skillfully orches-
trated, assume there will be no Muslim response to the lies, distortions, misrepresentations and fallacious arguments being spread about
Islam and Muslims. Unfortunately, far too many Muslims believe that
if they remain silent, keep a low profile and avoid any controversies
eventually all of the hatred and bigotry being directed at Muslims will
simply go away.

This is a terribly misguided belief. Muslim silence in articulating
the truth about our religion, our history in this country and the way
the events of 9/11 have affected our community only helps to create
a void that is being filled with falsehood. Eventually, in the absence of

a countervailing narrative, those falsehoods will come to be perceived as the truth. In the words of Norman Daniel:

> By misapprehension and misrepresentation, a notion of the ideas and beliefs of one society can pass into the accepted myths of another society, in a form so distorted that its relation to the original facts is sometimes barely discernable. Doctrines that are the expression of the spiritual outlook of an enemy are interpreted ungenerously and with prejudice, and even the facts are modified –and in good faith- to suit the interpretation. In this way is constituted a body of belief about what another group of people believes. A 'real truth' is identified: this is something that contrasts with what the enemy say they believe; they must not be allowed to speak for themselves. This doctrine about doctrine is widely repeated, and confirmed by repetition in slightly varying forms.[37]

The recent controversy around the Park51 Project in New York illustrates how this misrepresentation works at many different levels. The public frenzy surrounding that project has been fabricated on the basis of lies and distortion. The "Ground Zero Mosque" is not at ground zero. It is not a mosque, and the location it is to be built on is not "hallowed" ground. It is in a sleazy area populated by strip clubs, bars, smoke shops and liquor stores. The allegation that the former name of the project, "Cordova House" symbolizes Muslim conquest is also a lie. The name was chosen to reflect the tolerant culture Muslims, Christians and Jews were able to create in Andalusia. The city reverted to Christian control in 1248 AD and has remained under Christian rule since then. Hence, this would truly be a pathetic symbol of Muslim conquest, were that the intention of the organizers of the project.

A further argument is that the project is a "slap in the face" of Americans who lost almost three thousand of their fellow citizens at the site of the World Trade Center on that fateful day. There are two insidious assumptions embedded in this argument. The first is that

American Muslims are not "real" citizens. Hence, in the eyes of the anti-Muslim bigots, the lives lost that fateful day were "our" loss, not "theirs." From here it is a small leap to conclude that "we" have rights that can be denied to "them," because of "our" suffering.

The second is that no Muslims were killed that day. If there were, "we" reserve the right to define for Muslims what their deaths should mean. These arguments are a slap in the face of every American Muslim who was grief-stricken and traumatized that day, like so many of their countrymen. They are also an affront to all of the Muslims who died that day as well as their families. Many of the Muslims who lost family members in the collapsing towers have had to deal with the loss of their loved ones and the insults, humiliation, and threats occurring during the ensuing backlash.[38]

That Muslims died in the attack on the World Trade Center towers is undeniable. Here is a list of their names:

1. Shabbir Ahmed - 47 years old - Windows on the World Restaurant

2. Tariq Amanullah - 40 years old - Fiduciary Trust Co.

3. Michael Baksh - 36 years old - Marsh & McLennan

4. Touri Hamzavi Bolourchi - 69 years old - retired nurse on United #175

5. Abul K. Chowdhury - 30 years old - Cantor Fitzgerald

6. Mohammad Salahuddin Chowdhury - 38 years old - Windows on the World

7. Jemal Legesse De Santis - 28 years old - World Trade Center

8. Simon Suleman Ali Kassamali Dhanani - 63 years old - Aon Corp.

9. Syed Abdul Fatha - 54 years old - Pitney Bowes

10. Mon Gjonbalaj - 65 years old - Janitor, World Trade Center

11. Nezam A. Hafiz - 32 years old - Marsh & McLennan

12. Mohammed Salman Hamdani - 23 years old - NYPD Cadet

13. Zuhtu Ibis - 25 years old - Cantor Fitzgerald

14. Muhammadou Jawara - 30 years old - MAS Security

15. Sarah Khan - 32 years old - Forte Food Service

16. Taimour Firaz Khan - 29 years old - Carr Futures

17. Abdoulaye Kone - 37 years old - Windows on the World

18. Abdu Ali Malahi - 37 years old - WTC Marriott

19. Nurul Hoque Miah - 35 years old - Marsh & McLennan

20. Boyie Mohammed - 50 years old - Carr Futures

21. Ehtesham U. Raja - 28 years old - TCG Software

22. Ameenia Rasool - 33 years old - Marsh & McLennan

23. Mohammad Ali Sadeque - 62 years old - newspaper vendor at WTC, reported missing

24. Rahma Salie & child - 28 years old (7 months pregnant) - American #11

25. Khalid M. Shahid - 25 years old - Cantor Fitzgerald

26. Mohammed Shajahan - 41 years old - Marsh & McLennan

27. Nasima Hameed Simjee - 38 years old - Fiduciary Trust Co.

28. Michael Theodoridis - 32 years old - American #11

29. Abdoul Karim Traore - 41 years old - Windows on the World

30. Karamo Trerra - 40 years old - ASAP NetSource

31. Shakila Yasmin - 26 years old - Marsh & McLennan

The number of Muslims who died that day at the site of the World Trade center is a contentious issue. The number mentioned here is the most conservative count. This number[39], compared to the 2,752 people who perished in New York that day, mirrors the percentage of Muslims in the overall American population. Hence, by this measure, the loss to American Muslims that day was just as great as the loss suffered by the country at large,[40] if we choose to look at the issue in this divisive fashion.

In an ironic twist of fate, the first child born to a 9/11 widow was a Muslim; Farhad Chowdhury, the son of Mohammad S. Chowdhury, was born two days after the criminal attacks of 9/11. Are we to tell this child that his father's death is meaningless? Are we to tell him that because of his religion he is not entitled to all of the rights accruing to the Christians or Jews who perished on that awful day? Should we inform him that the site of the collapsing towers is not "hallowed" for him, even though his father perished there? I would think not. Therefore, in fighting for the rights of Muslims to build a masjid anywhere in this country, we are honoring the memory of Mohammad S. Chowdhury and all of the other Muslims who died that day.

It is also worth noting the existence of an informal mosque on the 17th floor of the south tower of the World Trade Center. That space was also destroyed in the attacks of 9/11.[41] This only emphasizes the fact that Muslims were a vital part of the life of the World Trade Center and as such should be a vital part of the future of the site and any memorials that are erected in honor of those who died there.

Our country is being usurped by lying warmongers who do not hesitate to distort the truth to serve their twisted agenda. It is time for us to stand up and say enough is enough. This country does not belong to the neo-fascists who are attempting to use fear of Islam to distract people from the suffering caused by neo-liberal economic policies, rapacious banks and the other realities conspiring to devastate the lives of hardworking, unsuspecting people. It belongs to its people, young and old, black and white, male and female, Muslim, Christian, Jew, Hindu and Buddhist. It will take a collective effort by all of us to make this country a more perfect union.

We are all in this together. We must join forces to begin the many serious discussions we need in order to put an end to the slow erosion of not only the foundation this country was built on, but the erosion of fundamental human dignity itself. Our coming together is the greatest tribute any of us could pay to the memory of those who perished on 9/11.

10.

POEMS

A Moment In Your Love

To spend a moment in your love,
  beyond this world of strife.
To know the beauty of your face,
  beyond the realms of life.

To pay the price you ask of us
  O Lord of life sublime!
To purge the darkness from our hearts
  within this brief lifetime.

As babes we enter on the path
  not knowing where it leads,

And then we fall into its snares…
our wounded hearts do bleed.

We struggle on despite the pain
our weapons known to all.
To wage the war within ourselves
surrounded by Earth's walls.

The walls of lust, of fear, of greed
that hem us from all sides.
We fight with love, with hope, with faith…
to slay the beast of pride.

Perhaps the blood will purge our pain,
our love anew to grow.
Perhaps our wounds will heal our scars.
Perhaps our faith will grow.

Perhaps we'll know a purer love,
beyond the fleeting nights…
and days we spend upon the path
that leads us to your light.

A Poetic Tribute to Muhammad Ali
Part One: Ali the Fighter

He floated like a butterfly and stung like a bee,
the greatest fighter the world has yet to see.

His opponents agree on one thing, they all got it right;
in the ring with Ali your life was in danger that night.

Had he lived in the time of Jack Johnson, Marciano, Joe Louis,
or Max Schmeling, his superiority over all of the former
would be telling.

Had he fought Tyson or Holyfield at the height of his career,
on the list of heavyweight champions their names would not appear.

If presidents could box he would have whupped Richard Nixon,
If reindeer could fight he would have been beat Donner and Blitzen!

For his right was full of power and his left was relentless,
he'd whup people so bad he'd have to seek his Lord's repentance.

So when you discuss who was the greatest heavyweight of all-time,
to mention any name other than Ali's is a crime!

Part Two: Ali the Man

With the grace of a butterfly and the tenacity of a bee,
he struck many a blow against injustice and inequality.

Coming of age in an era of legal segregation,
he came to symbolize the highest values of the nation.

Standing up for the truth, defying the warmongering throng,
he declared, "I ain't got no quarrel with them Vietcong!"

He refused to take up the gun and to pull the trigger,
quipping, "Ain't no Vietcong ever called me nigger!"

Knowing when to attack and when to retreat,
he brought an entire nation to its feet;

Not to cheer his exploits going down in the ring,
but to fall right in line with Malcolm and King.

Willing to give up his title, the money, the lights,
he dedicated himself to another fight.

The fight for truth and justice to liberate lands occupied,
by the highest court in the land his case would not be denied.

To fight that particular battle was not a mean feat,
but in the arena of life he would know no defeat.

With a heart made of gold and a spirit to match,
he was able to rebuild his life almost starting from scratch.

With the fuel of love and the flame of good,
he lit the fire of hope in the hearts of many boys and
girls in the 'hood.

Not knowing the word "I can't," he was never deterred,
and because of his example many dreams were not deferred.

Now slowed by the vicissitudes of time, far removed from his mountain camp,he will always be known as the people's champ.

ENDNOTES

[1] My position on a number of controversial issues has been stated at length, among other places in my book, *Scattered Pictures: Reflections of an American Muslim*, published in 2005 by the Zaytuna Institute, and a 4-CD set entitled, *Looking Back to Look Ahead*, produced by Zaytuna Institute in 2006.

[2] In the modern context, such an oath of protection may result from the acceptance of citizenship, residency permits, visas issued for tourism, study or work, and other well-known means.

[3] Muhammad Khayr Haykal, *al-Jihad wa'l Qital fi al-Siyasa al-Shar'iyya* (Beirut: Dar Ibn Hazm, 1417/1996), 3:1499.

[4] Haykal, 3:1502.

[5] Imam Ibn 'Abd al-Rahman ibn Muhammad ibn Qudamah al-Maqdisi, *al-Sharh al-Kabir 'ala Matn al-Muqni'* (Beirut: Dar al-Kitab al-'Arabi, 1372/1972), 10:555

[6] Imam Muhammad ibn Idris al-Shafi'i, Kitab al-Umm (Beirut: Dar al-Ma'rifa, nd), 4:248.

[7] Ibn Majah, no. 2341.

[8] Muhammad ibn Ahmad ibn Juzayy al-Kalbi, *Qawanin al-Ahkam al-Shar'iyya* (Beirut: Dar al-'Ilm li'l Malayin, 1374/1974), p. 165.

[9] Imam Muhammad ibn 'Ali al-Shawkani, *al-Sayl al-Jarrar* (Beirut: Dar al-Kutub al-'Ilmiyya, 1405/1985), 4:529.

[10] There are those who argue that the correct interpretation of this verse is the opposite of what is implied here. Namely, it was encouraging those who stayed away from a battle in order to mind their crops and cattle to go forth to the fray lest they be destroyed by the advancing enemy forces. However, Imam al-Shawkani and others argue that the meaning is contingent on the situation. While that meaning may be the one applicable to the occasion of the verse's revelation, to argue that the verse is discouraging involvement in foolhardy acts of desperation is also operative. This is so based on the interpretive principle, *al-'Ibra li 'Umum al-Lafdh, la li Khusus al-Sabab* (The applicability of a verse is based on the generality of its wording not on the specificity of its revelation).

[11] See Imam Ibn 'Abideen, *Radd al-Muhtar 'ala al-Durr al-Mukhtar* (Cairo: Matba' Khidaywi Isma'il, 1286), 3:337

[12] Haykal, 2:1008

[13] Imam Muhammad ibn Ahmad al-Sarkhasi, *Sharh al-Siyar al-Kabir* (Cairo: Jami' al-Makhtutat Jami' al-Duwal al-'Arabiyya, 1372/1972), 1:62.

[14] The Khawarij were a fanatical group who emerged in the early days of Islam. One of their well-known excesses was their declaring Muslims who disagreed with them to be outside the fold of Islam, and then making it lawful to kill them.

[15] This statement does not discount the existence of black or psychological operations that are undertaken against Muslim civilians by the security apparatuses of Western powers at war in the Muslim world, along with their agents and surrogates. However, it is undeniably true that an increasingly large number of the attacks against Muslim noncombatants are undertaken by other Muslims.

[16] Quoted in Ward Thomas, *The Ethics of Destruction: Norms and Force in International Relations* (Ithaca, London: Cornell University Press, 2001), 90.

[17] The transcendental nature of Muslim norms does not deny the human effort that went into translating those norms into policy. Hence, like their medieval Christian scholastic counterparts, Muslim theologians struggled to define the scope and limits of civilian immunity.

[18] For an insightful study of the generally peaceful nature of Islam's spread among non-Muslim peoples, and its respect for them see Professor Thomas Arnold, *The Spread of Islam in the World : A History of Peaceful Preaching* (New Delhi: Goodword Books, 2001).

[19] The most notable exception to this assertion is the Armenian Genocide that occurred in Ottoman Turkey in 1915. This controversial tragedy

occurred during the waning years of a Muslim world governed by a viable Islamic tradition, and after Turkey had been transformed into a nationalist, quasi Islamic state led by the Young Turks. By that time, the Sultan was a powerless figurehead. For most of the Ottoman reign Armenians were a self-governing minority that enjoyed the protection of the rulers in Istanbul.

[20] See Abdal-Hakim Murad, *Bombing Without Moonlight : The Origins of Suicidal Terrorism* (Bristol, England: Amal Press, 2008). Murad convincingly demonstrates how Muslims who engage in wanton attacks against civilians are merely extensions of a deeply-rooted history of such violence in western civilization. Likewise, he shows how Muslims who would justify such violence openly reject the Islamic tradition of patience and restraint in strategic affairs.

[21] See John Gray, *Al Qaeda and What It Means To Be Modern* (New York: The New Press, 2005). Gray argues that the philosophy of al-Qaeda owes more to the positivism of Saint-Simon and Comte, anarchism and nihilism than to any traditional Islamic influences, and its organizational structure is a reflection of 21st Century globalization.

[22] Their exceeding limits lies in the continuation of their murderous ways.

[23] Muhammad b. Ahmad al-Qurtubi, *al-jami' li ahkam al-Qur'an* (Beirut: Dar Ihya' al-Turath al-'Arabi, 1995), 3:147

[24] Muhammad b. 'Umar Fakhruddin al-Razi, *mafatih al-ghayb* (Beirut: Dar Ihya' al-Turath al-'Arabi, 1995), 4:344

[25] Ibid., 4:344

[26] Tirmidhi, 2910

[27] Zayn al-Din Abu al-Faraj 'Abd al-Rahman bin Rajab al-Hanbali, *Lata'if al-Ma'arif fima li Mawasim al-'Am min al-Wadha'if* (Damascus: Dar Ibn Kathir, 1416/1996), 316

[28] Ibid., 318

[29] Ibid., 318-319

[30] Ibid., 319

[31] Muslim, 817

[32] Neil Postman, *Technopoloy: The Surrender of Culture to Technology* (New York, NY: Vintage Books, 1992), 123-124

[33] The point being made here is not to diminish the transformative power of faith. However, the transformative power of language is more systematic

and subtle, usually more enduring than that brought about by conversion or other experiences that are associated with faith.

[34] See Toshihiko Izutsu, *Ethico-Religious Concepts in the Qur'an* (Kuala Lumpur: Islamic Book Trust, 2004). Particularly relevant to the discussion I am engaging in are chapters 3-6.

[35] Ibid., 295

[36] Mentioned by Imam al-Suyuti in *al-Durr al-Manthur*, see Jalal al-Din al-Suyuti, *al-Durr al-Manthur* (Beirut: Dar al-Ihya' al-Turath al-'Arabi, 1421/2001), 8:226-227.

[37] Norman Daniel, *Islam and the West: The Making of an Image* (Oxford, England: Oneworld, 2000), 12.

[38] Consider the following examples of such abuse. Salman Hamdani, a New York City police cadet who perished in the collapsed towers, while working to save the lives of others, was subsequently accused of being a terrorist. See http://usinfo.state.gov/products/pubs/humantoll/hamdani.htm (accessed 9/24/10). Family members of Rahma Salie were placed on a no fly list and not allowed to attend a memorial service for her.

See http://islam.about.com/od/terrorism/a/Muslim-Victims-Of-9-11-Attack.htm (accessed 9/24/10). Bahareen Ashrafi was taunted with calls, "Let's go for a Jihad." See http://www.people.com/people/archive/article/0,,20199602,00.html (accessed 9/24/10).

[39] This list is taken from the following website: http://islam.about.com/od/terrorism/a/Muslim-Victims-Of-9-11-Attack.htm (referenced 9/24/10). While the final number of Muslims who died in New York that day is debatable, some lists mention as many as 60 Muslims perishing that day, I prefer the more conservative figure.

[40] The small percentage of Muslims in the overall United States population belies the idea that there is an imminent threat of Muslims taking over America or being poised to impose "Shariah" law on the country. The tiny size and corresponding weakness of the Muslim population is one of the reasons it is being targeted and scapegoated the way that it is. There is little danger of any negative political, financial or physical consequences for the aggressing parties.

[41] See Samuel G. Freedman, "Muslims and Islam Were Part of the Tower's Life," *New York Times* (9/10/2010). http://www.nytimes.com/2010/09/11/nyregion/11religion.html.

www.ingramcontent.com/pod-product-compliance
Lightning Source LLC
Chambersburg PA
CBHW050559280326
41933CB00011B/1902